Fish Tricks

THE WILD & WACKY WORLD OF FISH

HAUDE LEVESQUE, PhD

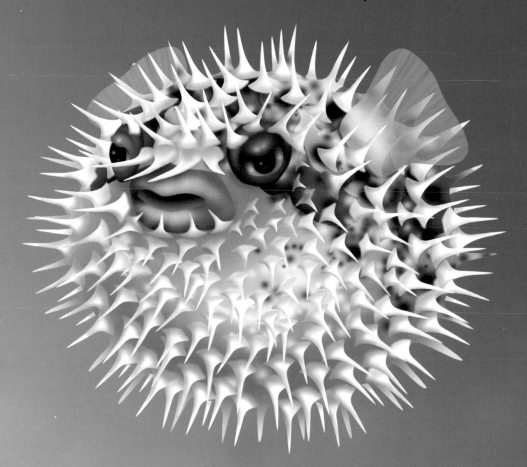

MoonDance

Quarto is the authority on a wide range of topics.
Quarto educates, entertains, and enriches the lives of our readers—
enthusiasts and lovers of hands-on living.
www.quartoknows.com

Produced by EarlyLight Books
Page Layout: Dawn Cusick
Proofreading: Meredith Hale

MoonDance

6 Orchard Road, Suite 100
Lake Forest, CA 92630
quartoknows.com
Visit our blogs @quartoknows.com

MIX
Paper from
responsible sources
FSC® C017606

Printed in China
1 3 5 7 9 10 8 6 4 2

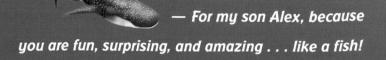

— For my son Alex, because you are fun, surprising, and amazing . . . like a fish!

Contents

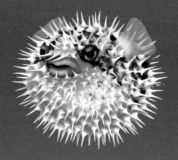

Introduction

Welcome to the amazing world of fish!

Most people find fish fascinating, perhaps because fish live in a world so different from our own. Fish were the first vertebrates to appear on Earth during the Cambrian period, 515 million years ago. Even though they have been here for millions of years, they could not be safely studied underwater until the 1940s, when two Frenchmen, Jacques-Yves Cousteau and Émile Gagnan, invented the Aqua-Lung used by scuba divers. We still do not know a lot about nocturnal fish and deep-sea fish.

Scientists who study fish are called ichthyologists (ICK-thee-ah-lo-gists). In the early 1970s, ichthyologists were surprised to learn more about fish building nests and burrows. The surprises continue! Some fish use rocks as tools to get food. Other fish use chemicals or sound to share information. To find food, fish use barbels, lures, and electricity. They even squirt water at land animals! To avoid predators, fish camouflage themselves as seaweed and sponges, and use toxins and spines. Some fish are good parents, too, taking good care of their eggs and fry.

I get really excited when I learn something new about animals, and I hope you feel the same way. (My secret life goal is to know all the animals on the planet. I know it's a foolish and impossible goal, but it's fun to try!) As you learn more about fish, I hope you will realize how important it is for people to protect fish and their habitats.

Maude Levesque

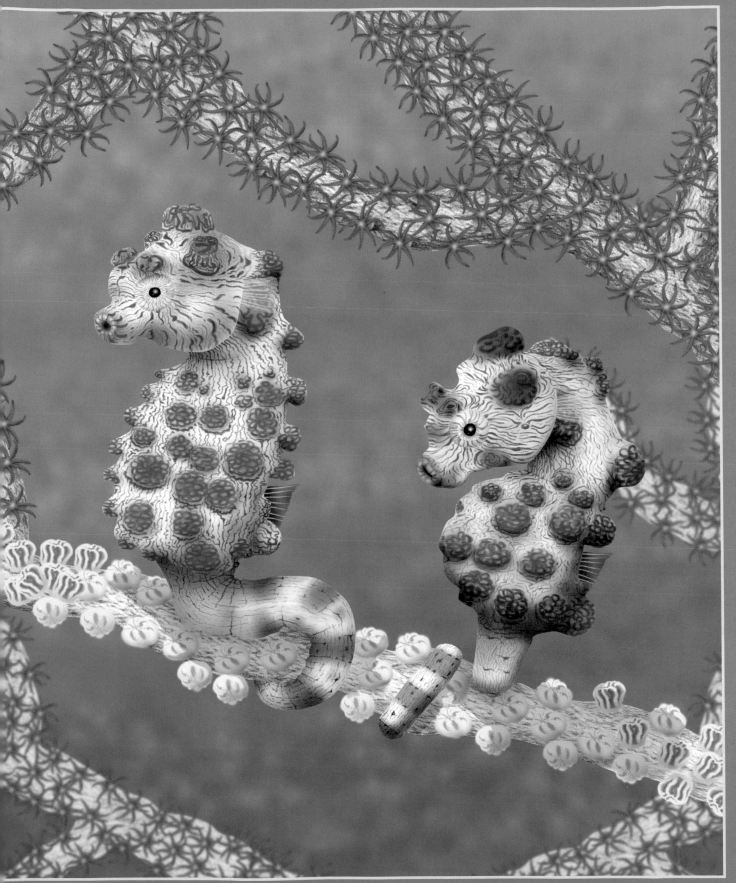

Meet the Fish

What Is a Fish?

Fish are animals that live in water and have gills, fins, and scales. This is a rough definition because there are many exceptions. Fish have two sets of paired fins and several unpaired fins. Like people, fish are vertebrates, which means they have vertebral columns that support their bodies and skulls to protect their brains. Mammals, reptiles, birds and amphibians are vertebrates, too.

Fish can be found all over the world in almost any place with water. Fish come in many sizes. Whale sharks can grow up to forty feet long, while pygmy seahorses are less than an inch long. There are more than 30,000 species of fish.

There are three main types of fish. The first type, the jawless fish, includes lampreys and hagfish. Instead of a jaw, these fish use an oral disc to latch on to prey.

The second group includes fish such as sharks and rays. These fish have skeletons made from cartilage instead of bones. You can feel cartilage by squeezing the outer part of your ear.

The third type of fish is called the bony fish because their skeletons are made from bones. Most fish are this type.

Scales grow from fish skin. They protect fish and help them swim faster by reducing water friction. There are five types of fish scales. They come in many sizes, depending on the type of fish and its age.

PLACOID SCALES

The scales on sharks and rays are tiny teeth that cover their whole body. These scales are called placoid scales, and they have enamel, dentine, and inner pulp just like your teeth. When sharks and rays grow, their scales do not grow with them and become spaced out over their body. New scales are always being made, though, and soon grow in the empty spaces between older scales.

The other four types of scales are found on bony fish. These scales grow with the fish in circular rings each year. Some fish biologists can use the rings to find out a fish's age. Cosmoid scales are only found in the fossils of some extinct fish and on a few living fish such as lungfish. Ganoid scales evolved from cosmoid scales. They are found on some ancient fish such as sturgeons, gars, and paddlefish. These interlocking bony scales work like a protective armor.

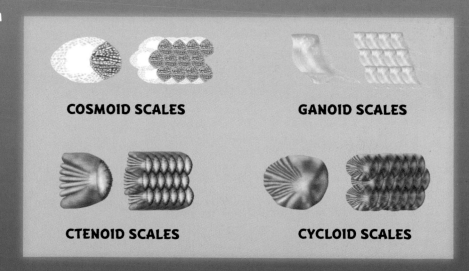

COSMOID SCALES

GANOID SCALES

CTENOID SCALES

CYCLOID SCALES

Most bony fish have ctenoid or cycloid scales, which are very similar. Some kinds of flat fish have two types of scales on their bodies! Very ancient fish, such as lampreys and hagfish, do not have scales. A few other fish, such as icefish, lost their scales as they adapted to their habitat.

Not Fish!

Not every animal that lives in water is a fish. Mammals such as whales, dolphins, walruses, seals, and otters live in water. Some reptiles such as sea snakes and turtles live in water, too. Many animals without backbones, called invertebrates, also live in water. Here is just a short list: octopuses, squid, snails, jellies, anemones, corals, sponges, lobsters, crabs, mussels, clams, oysters, sea stars, and sea urchins.

Fish Anatomy

Most fish use feather-like organs called gills to breathe. (A few fish have lungs.) Gills are held together with four or five gill arches on each side of a fish's head. Gill arches are protected by a skin flap called an operculum. Water flows in from the fish's mouth, across the gills, and out through the operculum. Oxygen in the water moves across the gills to the blood.

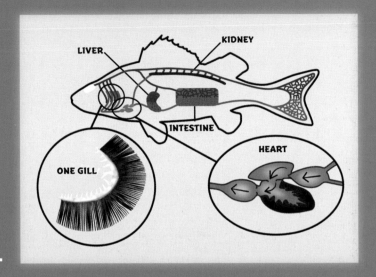

Fish use strong muscles that run from their gills to their tail to help them swim. A balloon-like swim bladder holds air and keeps them from sinking. Fish also have the same organs that most vertebrates have, including a heart, liver, kidneys, intestines, and a brain.

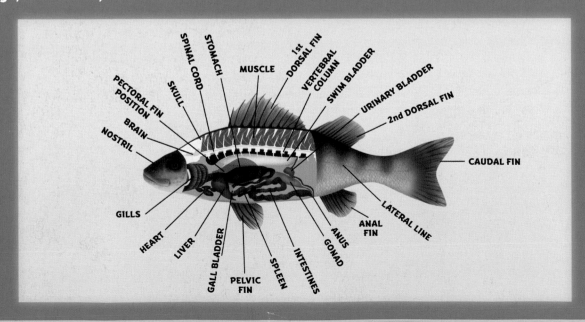

Fish eyes are a lot like human eyes. Both have a cornea, lens, pupil, iris, and retina in each eye. Humans and fish use rod cells and cone cells in their retinas to help them see. Rod cells work well in low light, and these cells only see black and white. Deep-sea fish and nocturnal fish have many rod cells. Like humans, fish see red, blue, and green light with cone cells. Some fish also have a fourth type of cone cell that lets them see ultraviolet light.

Fish eyes are different from human eyes in some important ways, though. First, fish do not have eyelids so their eyes are always open! Second, the iris in humans changes size to let more or less light into the retina. (The iris is the part of your eye that gives your eyes their color.) Other vertebrates that live on land have irises that work this way, too. In most fish, the iris stays the same size all the time because the light does not change as much underwater as it does on land. For close-up vision, eye muscles make human lenses rounder, while fish lenses move back and forth inside the eyeball.

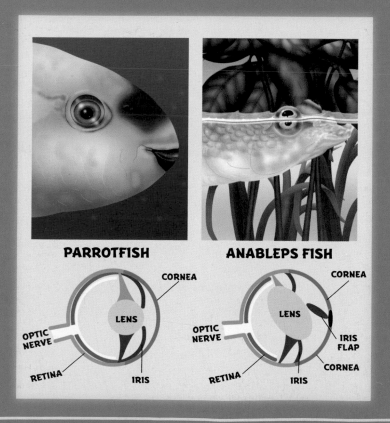

PARROTFISH   ANABLEPS FISH

CORNEA
LENS
OPTIC NERVE
RETINA   IRIS

CORNEA
LENS
OPTIC NERVE
IRIS FLAP
CORNEA
RETINA   IRIS

If you do just a little research, you can find some cool adaptations in fish eyes. The anableps fish, for example, is called the four-eyed fish. They do not really have four eyes, but they do have two irises and two corneas in each eye. These fish spend most of their time on the water's surface so they need eyes that work well in both air and water so they can see land and water predators. Anableps live in muddy streams and mangroves in South and Central America.

Fish Food

Like other animals, fish need food energy to survive. Some fish are herbivores, feeding on plants and algae. Other fish are carnivores that eat other animals. Animals that live in the same environment, or ecosystem, are part of the same food web. An ecosystem's food web shows which organisms are eating — and being eaten by — other organisms.

Food webs always start with plants, algae, or bacteria that can get energy directly from the sun instead of from other organisms. Plants are called primary producers in the food web. In aquatic habitats, grasses and algae only live in shallow, clear water that lets sunlight through.

Plankton is a major part of fresh and marine water food webs. The plants and animals that float on the surfaces of water make up plankton. Many animals that live at the bottoms of rivers, lakes, and oceans feed on plankton that falls down to them. The amount of plankton in an ecosystem affects how much food there is for all animals.

Plant plankton is called phytoplankton. (*Phyto* means light.) Phytoplankton is usually very small, and it is food for many kinds of animals. Animal plankton is called zooplankton. (*Zoo* means animal.) Zooplankton comes in many sizes, from small animal eggs and larvae to much larger animals such as jellies. Small animals that eat zooplankton are then eaten by larger fish.

Fish Sense

Sound Tricks

Most people are surprised to learn that some fish use sounds to talk to each other. Fish make sounds in several ways. The giant ocean sunfish grinds its teeth, while other fish grind their bones or rub the spines on their fins against their bodies, the way crickets make sounds by rubbing their legs over their wings. Fish use these sounds to distract predators, to attract mates, and to bring or keep schools together.

Male and female toadfish make grunting sounds by squeezing muscles on the sides of their swim bladders. Males also make long, whistle-like sounds when they build nests and compete for females. There are about eighty species (types) of toadfish and each species makes a different sound.

Smell & Taste Tricks

Fish use chemical smells and tastes to find food, avoid predators, and speak to each other. Some fish use chemicals to help them migrate, too. Instead of using their tongue for tasting, the way you do, fish taste with their fins, lips, and barbels. (Barbels are whisker-like growths near the mouths of some fish.)

Fish can smell a thousand times better than people! Their noses usually look like small dents in front of their eyes. The pits are lined with millions of receptors that can pick up smells. Fish that live in cloudy water use their sense of smell more than fish that live in clear water.

Catfish hold the record for having the best sense of taste of all vertebrate animals. This great sense of taste earned them the nickname "swimming tongue." Their extra-long barbels look like whiskers.

Alarm Tricks

Karl von Frisch, a famous German scientist, first reported alarm chemicals in minnows in the 1970s. Dr. von Frisch also discovered the waggle dance that bees use to tell other bees where to find food.

Minnows are small, freshwater fish that are common prey to bigger fish such as pike. Minnows do not have toxic spines, big teeth, or other ways to fight off predators, but they do have some very cool cells that help to warn other minnows that danger is nearby. When a minnow is under attack, club cells on the surface of their skin break open. Other minnows can smell these chemicals more than twelve feet away, giving them a chance to escape or hide when a predator is near.

DID YOU KNOW?

A minnow's alarm chemical can still be smelled after a predator has eaten it. Other minnows can even smell the chemical in a predator's feces. To keep minnows from knowing they are nearby, pike do not poop where they hunt.

Schooling Tricks

Some fish, such as these mackerels, spend all of their time in groups called schools that can have hundreds or even thousands of fish in them. Sometimes, a large school looks like a single, very large fish to a predator. Other times, the fast movements in a school can confuse or tire out a predator.

Have you ever watched a school quickly change directions and wondered why fish don't bump into each other? Fish use the same senses that people use — sight, sound, smell, touch, and taste — to help them school. They also use a sixth sense called lateral line that helps them know when nearby fish move.

DID YOU KNOW?

Lateral lines run down both sides of a fish's body. The line is made from a row of small pores that have a water canal under them that help fish feel very small changes in the speed and direction of water movement. Most fish also have small pores on their face that work the same way.

Electricity Tricks

Some fish can make electricity that is strong enough to shock prey and fight off predators. Amazonian electric eels, African catfish, and torpedo rays use electricity this way. Another group of fish makes weak electrical currents. The elephant-nose fish, for example, uses a weak electrical field around its body to know when it's near animals or objects. Fish that live in cloudy water and nocturnal fish use these kinds of electrical fields to know what's around them. The South American knifefish uses small amounts of electricity to make signals that attract females.

How do fish make electricity? They use electric organs that are filled with a special type of muscle cell. These cells are called electrocytes: *electro* means electricity and *cyte* means cell. Each electrical organ is made from hundreds of columns of stacked electrocytes that work like batteries stacked end to end.

DID YOU KNOW?
Ancient Greeks used electric rays to numb pain during operations and childbirth.

Torpedo rays such as the one shown here have kidney-shaped electrical organs on the sides of their head. In electric eels and catfish, the electrical organs are near the back of their bodies. Some types of torpedo rays release up to 200 volts at a time, which is enough to stun a human.

Great Adaptations

Lure Tricks

In the deep ocean, meals are hard to find. Some deep-sea fish prefer to wait for prey or pieces of food rather than spend time and energy searching for it. The deep-sea anglerfish lives up to 3,000 feet below the ocean's surface, where it is very dark. Compared to their body size, anglerfish have a large mouth and huge teeth. Their expandable jaws and stretchy stomachs let them eat very large prey.

Female anglerfish use a glowing lure called an esca to attract prey. The esca is filled with bacteria that make a blue-green light. Anglerfish can move their lures, and can even make their glowing lights flash. Scientists think that the lure can mimic small prey such as shrimp, which attracts larger prey.

DID YOU KNOW?

Each anglerfish species has its own type of filaments and barbels on its lure. Some anglerfish keep their lure inside their mouth!

Male anglerfish are very small, even as adults. They do not have glowing lures and cannot feed on their own. Instead, they live as parasites, attached to females. This adaptation helps when it's time to reproduce because there are so few anglerfish in the deep sea that it would be hard for them to find each other at the right time.

Hiding Tricks

Seadragons and some other fish use extra body parts to help them blend in with their habitat. Leafy seadragons look like the floating seaweed they live in.

Seadragons are in the seahorse family. They have long snouts and bodies, and do not have pelvic fins. They have small pectoral and dorsal fins that help them move, but they do not swim much.

Changing Tricks.

In habitats with clear water, such as coral reefs or tropical lakes, the most common fish colors are yellow and blue. In habitats where the water is not clear, most fish are black and white. During breeding season, some fish also have contrasting colors such as red or orange. These colors tell other fish in their species their age and sex, and they go away when breeding season ends.

Some fish change their patterns and colors as they get older. Young emperor angelfish look so different from adults that for a long time many biologists thought they were two different species! Adult emperor angelfish are very colorful. They eat sponges and algae. The young fish do not live near adults. They eat the mucus of other fish, such as moray eels. Their black stripes help them hide.

Camo Tricks

Fish use many types of camouflage to help them hide. You probably already know about animals with patterns and colors that help them blend in with their environment. Many animals that use camouflage also change the way they behave. For example, some fish look and behave like floating sticks, grasses, leaves, and even sponges.

Predators such as this frogfish look like sponges. When prey fish get close, the frogfish darts forward and eats them. These kinds of predators are called sit-and-wait predators and ambush predators. Frogfish are in the same family as the deep-sea anglerfish on pages 32 and 33.

Using camouflage is harder for prey fish because they need to move around while searching for food and mates.

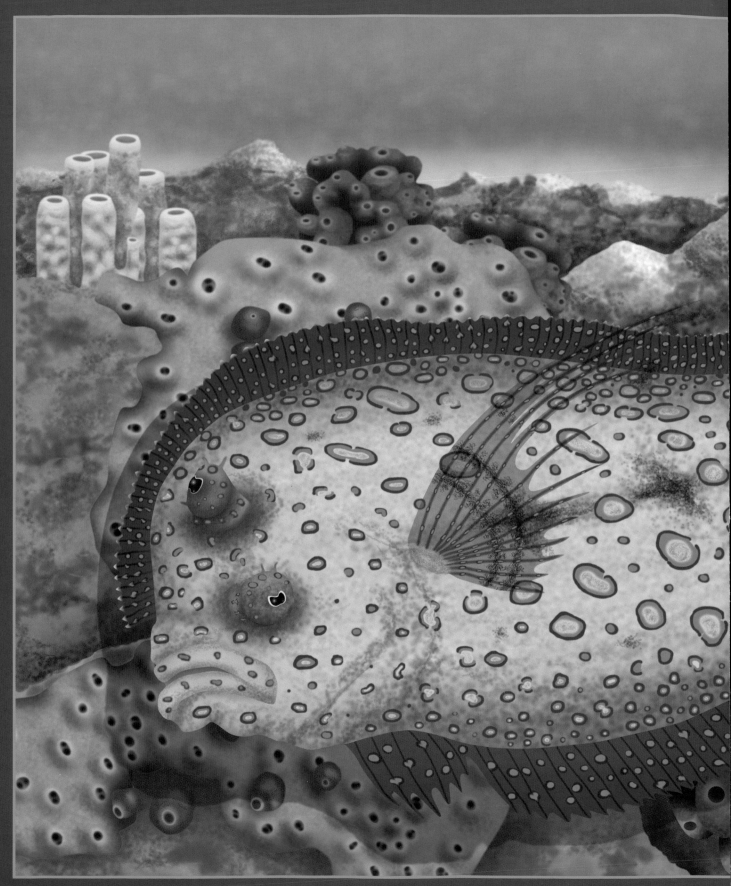

Color Tricks

Some flatfish can change colors very fast, which helps them blend in better with their backgrounds. Flounders that live on the sea floor, such as this peacock flounder, can copy the colors and patterns of nearby corals, sponges, and even the sea floor.

Fish have many types of color cells. (Humans have only one.) Some color cells make reds, yellows, blues, and blacks. Other color cells add the silvery shine that some fish have. Hormones and other signals from the fish's brain control colors and their brightness.

DID YOU KNOW?

Color cells are called chromatophores. *Chromo* means color and *phore* means part.

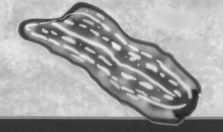

Tool Tricks

How many tools do you use every day? A pencil for math homework? A toothbrush for cleaning your teeth? A spoon for eating cereal? Biologists used to believe that only humans used tools, but now they know that primates, dolphins, elephants, birds, and even octopuses use tools, too.

In 2006, a professional diver heard a strange noise while underwater. When he swam over to check it out, he found a blackspot tuskfish smashing a clam against a rock. When the clam's shell broke open, the tuskfish ate it. Luckily, the diver had his underwater camera with him and recorded the first proof that fish can use tools.

The diver also noticed many shell pieces around the rock, so this wasn't the fish's first tool use. The blackspot tuskfish is a type of wrasse that lives on Australia's Great Barrier Reef and can grow up to three feet long. Since then, biologists have learned that a few other types of wrasse use tools to break open clams, mussels, scallops, oysters, and sea urchins. Some wrasse use rocks the same way the blackspot tuskfish does. Other wrasse throw their prey at the rock.

DID YOU KNOW?

Water is thicker than air so it takes more energy to move tools through water. Don't believe it? Take an apple into a pool and throw it as hard as you can underwater. How far did it go? Now throw the same apple on land in the same way. Did it go farther?

Water Jet Tricks

Can fish use water as a tool? Maybe! The archerfish that live in tropical mangrove swamps in India and Australia eat insects that live on plants near the water's surface. To catch a bug, an archerfish aims a jet of water at it. When the bug falls off the plant and into the water, the archerfish eats it.

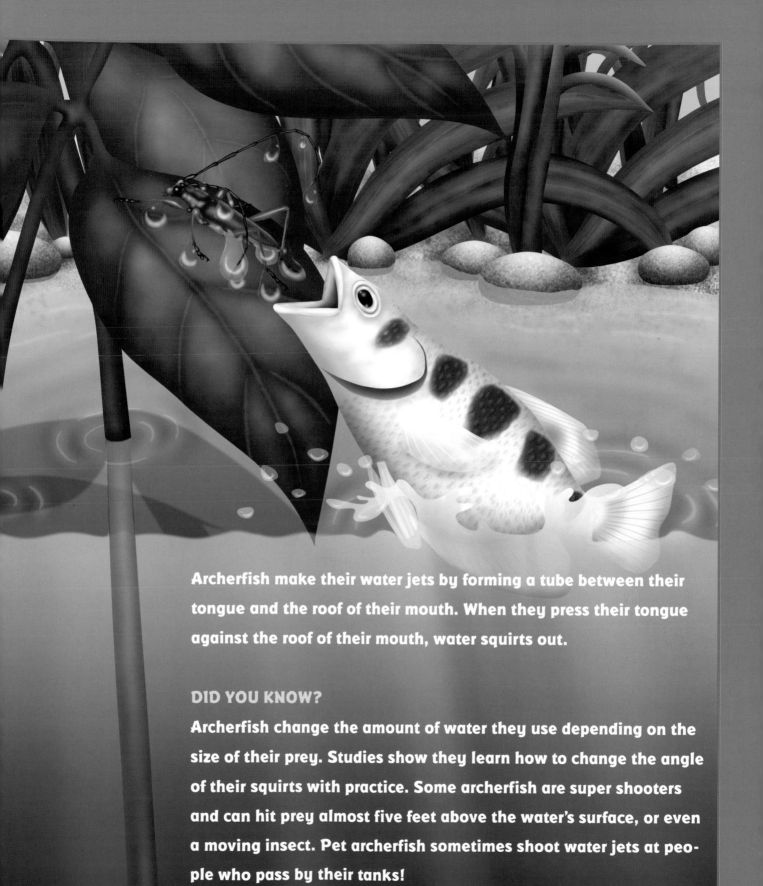

Archerfish make their water jets by forming a tube between their tongue and the roof of their mouth. When they press their tongue against the roof of their mouth, water squirts out.

DID YOU KNOW?

Archerfish change the amount of water they use depending on the size of their prey. Studies show they learn how to change the angle of their squirts with practice. Some archerfish are super shooters and can hit prey almost five feet above the water's surface, or even a moving insect. Pet archerfish sometimes shoot water jets at people who pass by their tanks!

Feeding Tricks

Triggerfish eat a lot of sea urchins, and they do it in a very cool way. Sea urchins are bottom feeders so their mouths are on their undersides. They do not have any spines around their mouths, which leaves this part of their body unprotected. To flip a sea urchin upside down, a triggerfish blows on it.

DID YOU KNOW?

Triggerfish live in the shallow
waters of tropical seas. Their sharp,
cutting teeth help them feed on snails, crabs,
shrimp, sea urchins, and other marine animals.

Cleaning Tricks

Fish live in water, so you might think they would always be super clean. Water does not clean off the dead scales, old mucus, and parasites that can make fish sick, though, so it's important that fish find ways to get clean. Some fish go to special places called cleaning stations to be cleaned by smaller fish. The cleaner fish eat the dead scales, mucus, and parasites from the larger fish, called client fish.

Cleaning stations could be dangerous places if client fish started eating their cleaner fish, or if the cleaner fish were to eat the larger fish's healthy scales instead of dead ones. Instead, both fish cooperate with each other and both benefit. This type of relationship between two animals is called mutualism.

Cleaning Tricks

Many client fish spy on cleaning wrasse to find out whether wrasse are eating more than parasites and dead skin. How does a client fish know what a cleaning fish is eating? If a cleaner eats living skin or mucus, its client fish will jolt. Cleaner wrasse caught cheating may not get many new clients.

DID YOU KNOW?

There are many kinds of cleaning fish, including wrasse, cichlids, catfish, and gobies. There are even a few species of shrimp that are cleaners. One type of fish, the sabre-toothed blenny, looks and acts like cleaner wrasse but feeds on healthy scales and mucus.

Suction Cup Tricks

How would you like a suction pad on your head? You could stick yourself to anything — the bottom of a Ferris wheel chair or your classroom's ceiling — just by placing the top of your head against it! Believe it or not, the common remora fish has a suction pad on top of its head! The pad is a modified dorsal fin that has changed over a very long time. When a remora fish wants to attach itself, it presses the pad against a host and raises slats formed by strips of skin, creating a very strong suction force. In addition to fish, common remoras have been found attached to marine mammals, turtles, and sometimes even ships!

Living on another animal helps remoras in several ways. The remoras get food, transportation, and protection from predators. Living on a large animal also helps bring fast-moving water over their gills. Remoras can live on other animals for a few months. They can change places many times if they do not feel safe. Remoras do not help or hurt the animals they live on. This type of relationship is called a commensal symbiosis.

DID YOU KNOW?

In some parts of the world, people used remoras to catch sharks and turtles. After catching a remora, they would tie a rope to its tail and release it back into the sea. When the remora attached to an animal, it was pulled back into the fishing boat by the rope with a turtle or large fish attached!

Defense Tricks

How do you escape hungry predators if you cannot swim very fast? If you're a pufferfish, you inflate yourself like a water balloon so you're hard to swallow. To blow up their bodies, pufferfish quickly swallow lots of water to fill their large, stretchy stomachs. Like most adaptations, this one is not perfect. It takes a lot of energy for pufferfish to inflate their bodies, and they need a few hours to recover.

Some pufferfish species have large spines all over their bodies, which make them even less appetizing to predators. Pufferfish live in tropical waters around the world.

DID YOU KNOW?

In Japan, pufferfish meat is considered a treat called fugu. The meat must be fixed by chefs who have been trained to know which parts and how much of the pufferfish is safe to eat. Just one of these pufferfish is toxic enough to kill thirty people!

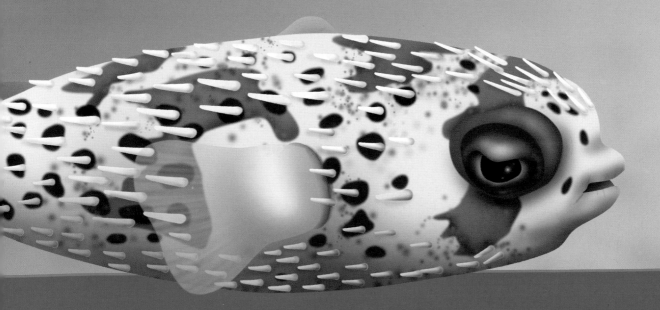

Blood Tricks

Here's a mystery for you. How do fish live in the freezing cold waters near Antarctica without freezing to death? Only a few types of fish can live in these waters.

Blackfin icefish and some other Antarctic fish use special proteins to lower the freezing point of their blood. These proteins are called antifreezes, and they stop ice crystals from forming or growing in fish blood.

Icefish have some other adaptations that help them survive in Antarctic waters. Because there is so much oxygen in the cold Antarctic waters, icefish get oxygen through their skin instead of through gills. They do not have many scales and their blood vessels are just under their thin skin. These fish do not have red blood cells so their blood is clear instead of red. Their blood is also very thin.

Partner Tricks

When clownfish live with sea anemones, both animals benefit. The clownfish get free food when they eat the anemone's leftovers, and the anemone's stinging tentacles give the clownfish some protection from predators. (Clownfish have special mucus that protects them from anemone stings.) Clownfish defend and clean the anemones they live in, and their swimming fins bring extra oxygen to the anemones.

Clownfish lay their eggs on a rock near their anemone. After the larvae hatch, they go through a free-swimming stage before they find their own anemone by smell.

When two or more animals live closely together, it is called a symbiosis. Because both the clownfish and the anemones benefit from their partnership, their type of symbiosis is called mutualism.

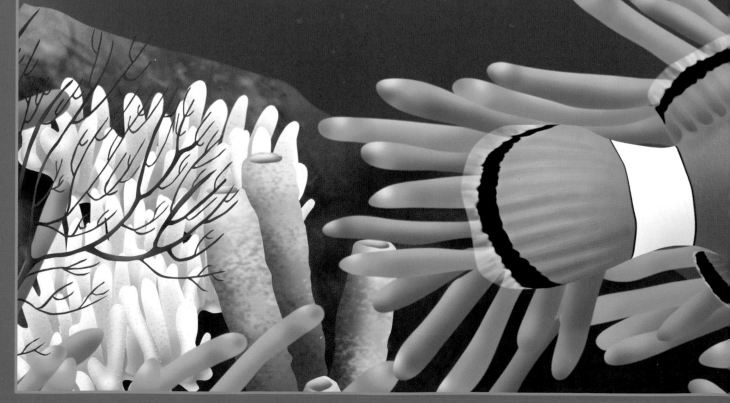

DID YOU KNOW?

Clownfish can change their gender from male to female one time. They live in small groups with one breeding pair and a few younger fish that work as helpers. At birth, all clownfish are males. The larger males become females, and defend the territory. If the female dies, the largest male becomes female.

Breathing Tricks

Just like other animals, fish need oxygen to live. Most fish only get their oxygen from water, using their gills, but a few fish can get it from the air. Some air-breathing fish use their skin to breathe, while others use their swim bladders or lung-like sacs. Most air-breathing fish live in water and come to the surface to gulp air. A few air-breathing fish can live on land when oxygen levels in water are low or when water dries up.

Mudskippers are a family of over twenty-five fish species. They are all air breathers and live in tropical areas such as mangroves and swamps. These fish can spend several hours out of the water. To survive, they need to stay moist so they have special mucus on their scales and roll themselves in mud.

Mudskippers breathe through their skin, mouths, and throats. (Salamanders and frogs breathe this way, too, because they have very small lungs.) Mudskippers have extra-strong pectoral and pelvic fins that help them move over the mud. Their gills are smaller and thicker than the gills in water-breathing fish, which keeps them from collapsing when the mudskippers are on land.

DID YOU KNOW?

Some mudskipper species build amazing burrows where they hide underwater and protect their eggs. To build a burrow, they use their mouths to take out mud and bring in fresh air. They have to re-build their burrows after every tide!

Fish Parents

Egg Tricks

Fish life starts with a fertilized egg. These eggs hatch into larvae that may look very different from their parents. Larvae still have an egg sac that they will use for food for a few days, and their fins do not work yet. Larvae change into fry, which look like small adults. Some types of fish give birth to small fish instead of spawning eggs.

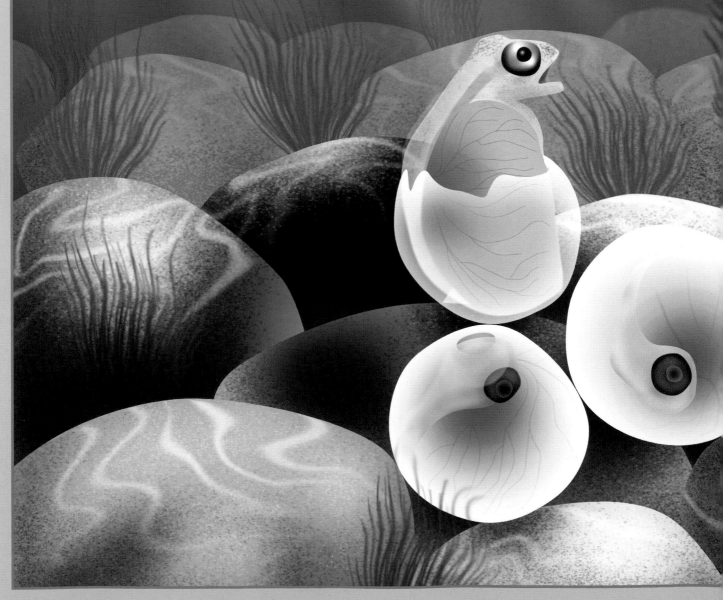

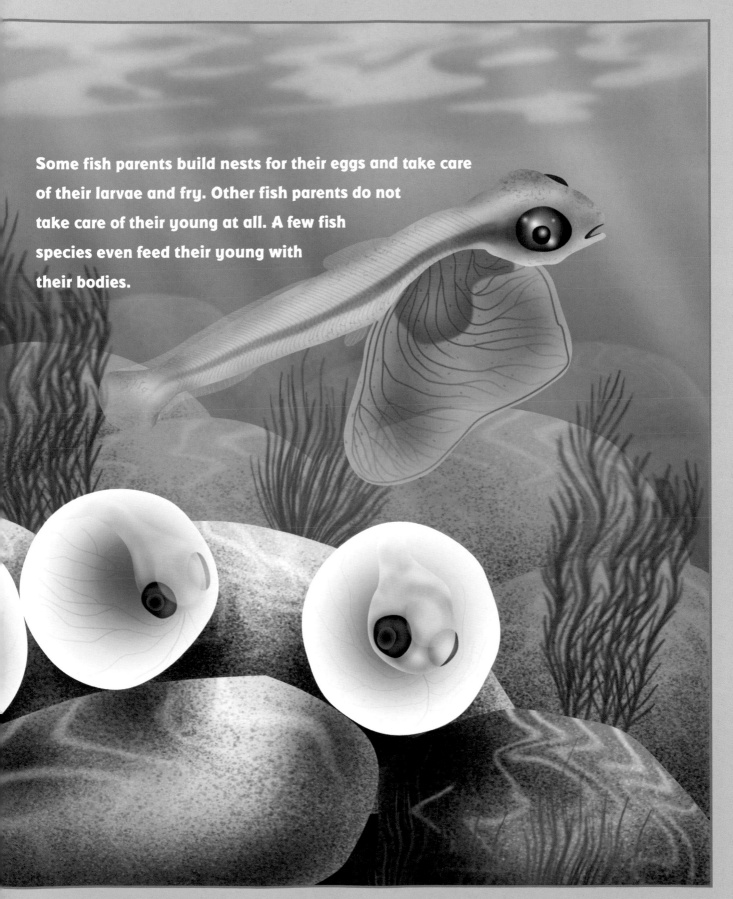

Some fish parents build nests for their eggs and take care of their larvae and fry. Other fish parents do not take care of their young at all. A few fish species even feed their young with their bodies.

Travel Tricks

Some fish migrate when it's time to reproduce because their larvae need different foods or habitats than the adults. The Chinook salmon shown here migrate and reproduce only once in their lifetime. Other fish, such as the Atlantic sturgeon, migrate every year.

In North America, Chinook salmon travel hundreds of miles from the ocean to fresh-water streams along the Pacific Northwest coastline. Once spawned, fertilized

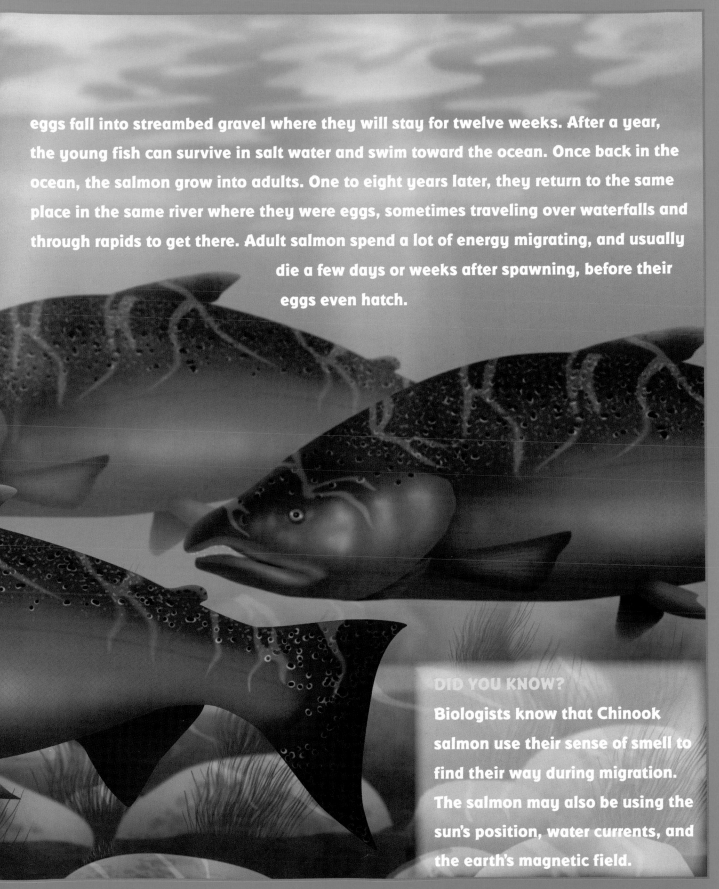

eggs fall into streambed gravel where they will stay for twelve weeks. After a year, the young fish can survive in salt water and swim toward the ocean. Once back in the ocean, the salmon grow into adults. One to eight years later, they return to the same place in the same river where they were eggs, sometimes traveling over waterfalls and through rapids to get there. Adult salmon spend a lot of energy migrating, and usually die a few days or weeks after spawning, before their eggs even hatch.

DID YOU KNOW?

Biologists know that Chinook salmon use their sense of smell to find their way during migration. The salmon may also be using the sun's position, water currents, and the earth's magnetic field.

Tunnel Tricks

In the spring, male three-spined stickleback fish search for a good place to build a nest. Their chins and abdomens turn red, and the irises in their eyes turn blue. The kidneys in male three-spined stickleback fish also start making a glue-like substance called spiggin.

To build a nest, the males dig small holes in the sand of coastal waters. Next, they look for pieces of soft algae that are just the right color. They make a barrel-shaped mass with the algae, and then push a hole in the middle with their snouts to form a tunnel. Last, they use spider web-like threads of spiggin from their kidneys to hold the algae in place.

Females choose a male by how bright his breeding colors are and what his nest looks like. After she lays her eggs in the nest, the female leaves. When breeding season is over, the males lose their bright colors and their kidneys stop making spiggin.

DID YOU KNOW?

Male three-spined sticklebacks spend all of their time taking care of the eggs and do not even leave their nest to eat. They rebuild any tares in their nest and remove fungus. They also fan the eggs with their fins all day and all night to keep lots of oxygen around them.

Nest Tricks

In 1995, a Japanese diver found a mystery on the sea floor: a large, perfectly shaped circle that looked like the crop circles people find on land. Years later, biologists learned the six-feet-wide circles were made by a five-inch-long fish!

Male white-spotted pufferfish take about nine days to build a nest. To carve grooves into the sand, they swim over it at different speeds while moving their fins. After carving the nest, they decorate the grooves with shellfish.

Females lay their eggs in the middle of the nest, where the finest sand is. Males take care of the eggs by cleaning and blowing on them until they hatch. Every year, males build new nests instead of re-using old ones.

Biologists who study these fish have noticed that female pufferfish prefer larger nests with more grooves and finer sand in the center. The grooves may protect the eggs from water currents. The shellfish and the grooves may also help protect young fish from predators.

Pufferfish in nest

Mouth Tricks

Instead of building nests to protect their eggs, some fish keep their fertilized eggs in their mouths. This behavior is called mouth brooding. In some species, such as the blue Zaire cichlid fish shown here, only the females mouth brood. In other species, only the males do it. In still other species, both males and females care for their eggs this way. While they are mouth brooding, parents turn their eggs around a lot to make sure they get enough oxygen. They usually do not eat until their eggs hatch.

Some fish keep mouth brooding after their eggs hatch. Young fish can leave their parent's mouth for short trips, but they stay nearby, swimming in groups. When parents sense danger, they move their heads or fins to tell their young fish to come back. When the fish get close to their parent's mouth, they are sucked back in!

DID YOU KNOW?

Some cichlid parents dig small pits before their eggs hatch. When their eggs hatch, they move their larvae to the pits where they are fanned and guarded. Sometimes the parents dig new pits and move their young to the new pits in their mouths.

Some discus fish parents release rich mucus from their skin to feed their fry for a few weeks. Discus fish are a type of cichlid fish.

Moving Tricks

The banded acara is a freshwater fish from South America that lays its sticky eggs on loose leaves instead of in nests. Both parents carefully choose the leaf. If a predator gets too close, the parents grab the edges of the leaf with their mouths and swim away with it! Both parents clean the eggs and fan them with their fins. They take turns leaving the eggs to feed or chase away predators.

DID YOU KNOW?

Some species of fish attach their eggs to their bodies. The banjo catfish carries its eggs outside on their abdomen, while the male seahorse uses a breeding pouch similar to a kangaroo pouch. The bitterling, a type of small carp, places its eggs inside a living mussel! Bitterling larvae leave the mussel after hatching.

Takeover Tricks

Like many types of fish, the venomous lionfish does not take care of its eggs, larvae, or fry. Instead, females release about a million eggs twice a year. The eggs float to the water's surface. Lionfish larvae and fry live on the surface as part of plankton, and many become food for larger animals.

Lionfish are known for the strong toxins in their spines. They are an invasive species in some parts of the world, and can take away food and habitat from many local fish.

Glossary

CARNIVORE: An organism that eats animals

CHEMICAL: A molecule made from atoms that interacts in organisms and the environment

ECOSYSTEM: A community of organisms and the environment they live in

FRY: Young fish

HABITAT: The home for an organism or a group of organisms

HERBIVORE: An organism that eats plants

HORMONE: A molecule secreted inside an organism that sends information from one area to another

ICHTHYOLOGIST: A scientist who studies fish behavior, morphology, and/or physiology

INVASIVE SPECIES: A species that enters a new habitat and causes damage to native organisms

INVERTEBRATE: An animal that does not have a backbone such as an insect, sea urchin, or clam

LARVA/LARVAE (singular/plural): Fish that have recently hatched from their egg

MUCUS: A slimy substance made from water and the protein mucin

MUTUALISM: A symbiotic relationship in which two or more organisms both benefit from each other

PARASITE: An organism that uses other organisms for food and habitat

PREDATOR: An organism searching for other organisms to eat

PROTEIN: A complex molecule made from hundreds of thousands of amino acids

SIGNAL: Information shared by one organism with another

SPAWNING: Releasing or depositing eggs

SPECIES: A group of organisms that live together in the wild and produce fertile offspring

SYMBIOSIS: Two or more organisms living closely together

TOXIN: A substance produced by organisms to help defend themselves from predators or to help them kill prey

VERTEBRATE: An animal that has a backbone such as a fish, bird, or mammal

Explore More!

CHECK OUT the following websites to learn more about fish and their habitats.
   www.dosits.org
   www.fishandkids.msc.org/en
   www.oceana.org/marine-life
   www.whoi.edu/know-your-ocean
   www.ocean.si.edu
   www.marinebio.org

Sources

G. Altomonte, O. Arakawa, C. Brown, S. Bruno, D. Coppola, G. Di Prisco, M. L. Fine, D. Giordano, D. F. Hwang, A. Ida, A. Ishimatsu, K. Ito, I. Karplus, H. Kawase, H. J. Lie, Y. Okata, S. Reebs, R. Russo, T. Takatani, S. Taniyama, F. Thorson, C. Verde, J. Q. Wilson, R. Wilson, www.dosits.org, and www.mudskipper.it

Scientific Names of Featured Animals

Page 1: Pufferfish *(Diodon hystrix)*

Pages 2-3: Gulf toadfish *(Opsanus beta)* and whale shark *(Rhincodon typus)*

Pages 4-5: Humpback anglerfish *(Melanocetus johnsonii)*, pufferfish *(Diodon hystrix)* and white-spotted pufferfish *(Torquigener albomaculosus)*, clown frogfish *(Antennarius maculatus)*, and hammerhead shark *(Sphyrna mokarran)*

Pages 6-7: Pygmy seahorses *(Hippocampus bargibanti)*

Pages 8-9: Whale shark *(Rhincodon typus)* and small golden trevally *(Gnathanodon speciosus)*

Pages 10-11: Sea lamprey *(Petromyzon marinus)*, hammerhead shark *(Sphyrna mokarran)*, yellow fin tuna *(Thunnus albacares)*, and channel catfish *(Ictalurus punctatus)*

Pages 12-13: Two-spotted octopus *(Octopus bimaculatus)* and bottlenose dolphin *(Tursiops* sp.), and green sea turtle *(Chelonia mydes)*

Pages 14-15: Yellow perch *(Perca flavescens)*

Pages 16-17: Phytoplankton (diatoms, dinoflagellates) and zooplankton (radiolarians, foraminiferans, and sea urchin, crab, and snail larvae)

Pages 18-19: Fathead minnows *(Pimephales promelas)* and Northern pike *(Esox lucius)*

Pages 20-21: Gulf toadfish *(Opsanus beta)*

Pages 22-23: Channel catfish *(Ictalurus punctatus)*

Pages 24-25: Fathead minnows *(Pimephales promelas)* and Northern pike *(Esox lucius)*

Pages 26-27: Atlantic mackerel *(Scomber scombrus)*

Pages 28-29: Bullseye electric ray *(Diplobatus ommata)*

Pages 30-31: Seven-spots archerfish *(Toxotes chatareus)*

Pages 32-33: Humpback anglerfish *(Melanocetus johnsonii)* and lanternfish *(Myctophum affine)*

Pages 34-35: Leafy seadragon *(Phycodurus eques)*

Pages 36-37: Adult emperor angelfish *(Pomacanthus imperator)* and young emperor angelfish *(Pomacanthus imperator)*

Pages 38-39: Clown frogfish *(Antennarius maculatus)* and flatworm *(Pseudoceros* sp.)

Pages 40-41: Peacock flounder *(Bothus mancus)* and flatworm *(Pseudoceros* sp.)

Pages 42-43: Blackspot tuskfish *(Choerodon schoenleinii)*

Pages 44-45: Seven-spots archerfish *(Toxotes chatareus)*

Pages 46-47: Bluelined triggerfish *(Pseudobalistes fuscus)*, sea urchin *(Diadema setosum)*, and green sea turtle *(Chelonia mydes)*

Pages 48-49: Bluestreak cleaner wrasse *(Labroides dimidiatus)* and cleaning bullethead parrotfish *(Chlorurus spilurus)*

Pages 50-51: Bluestreak cleaner wrasse *(Labroides dimidiatus)* and cleaning spotted moray eel *(Gymnothorax moringa)*

Pages 52-53: Remora *(Echeneis naucrates)* attached to tiger shark *(Galeocerdo cuvier)*

Pages 54-55: Pufferfish *(Diodon hystrix)*

Pages 56-57: Blackfin icefish *(Chaenocephalus aceratus)*

Pages 58-59: Common clownfish *(Amphiprion ocellaris)* and sea anemone *(Heteractis magnifica)*

Pages 60-61: Mudskipper *(Periophthalmus chrysospilos)*

Pages 62-63: Blue Zaire cichlid *(Cyphotilapia gibberosa)*

Pages 64-65: Atlantic salmon *(Salmo salar)*

Pages 66-67: Chinook salmon *(Oncorhynchus tshawytscha)*

Pages 68-69: Three-spined stickleback *(Gasterosteus aculeatus)*

Pages 70-71: White-spotted pufferfish *(Torquigener albomaculosus)*

Pages 72-73: Blue Zaire cichlid *(Cyphotilapia gibberosa)*

Pages 74-75: Banded acara *(Bujurquina vittata)*

Pages 76-77: Lionfish *(Pterois volitans)*

Index